My Favorite Bible Stories

Originally written by Allan Jahsmann for Concordia Bible Lessons

Selected and arranged by Lillian Brune

Concordia Publishing House, St. Louis, Missouri

Concordia Publishing House, St. Louis, Missouri

© 1967 Concordia Publishing House

Library of Congress Catalog Card No. 67-15957

MANUFACTURED IN THE UNITED STATES OF AMERICA

Contents

How God Made All Things

Genesis 1:1-25

A long time ago there was no beautiful world. There was no sun, no moon. There were no trees, no rivers, no grass, no animals, no birds, no people. There was only God.

Then God made the world. He made it out of nothing. This is how He made it beautiful. First He said, "Let there be light," and there was light. Then He divided the light from the darkness. And He called the darkness night and the light day.

Next God made the earth and the sky. He just told the soft clouds to float across the sky, and there they were, just as they are today. Then He made the rivers and the blue lakes and the big wide ocean. He also made the dry land, the hills, and the fields.

After this God covered the earth with lovely green grass. Everywhere pretty flowers sprang up. God also made big trees. Some were fruit trees loaded with apples and peaches and pears and cherries.

From the ground God also made wheat and oats and corn and many kinds of vegetables grow. He wanted His children to have plenty of food for themselves and the animals.

Next God wanted some pretty lights in the sky. So He made the sun and the moon and many, many stars. He said the sun should shine in the daytime and the moon and the stars should shine at night.

God saw that everything He had made was very good. The earth was a beautiful place, but everything was quiet. There were no living things. So God made fish to swim in the water and birds to sing in the trees. He also made kittens and rabbits and lions and elephants and all kinds of butterflies and bugs. God made all the living things on earth.

When God had finished, He was pleased with everything He had made. Everything was very good and just as He wanted it to be.

The First People

Genesis 2:4-25

God wanted someone to enjoy all the good things He had made. He wanted someone to thank and praise Him for what He had done. So God made a man. He called the man Adam. For Adam, God made a very special garden. It was to be his home.

The garden was like a park. There was grass and there were fruit trees. Lots of good fruit grew on these trees so that Adam could eat when he was hungry. A river gave Adam good cold water so that he could drink when he was thirsty. Pretty birds flew among the trees and sang happily. God also put animals into the garden.

Adam wasn't afraid of the lions and bears, for they weren't wild at first. They liked Adam and would not harm him. God brought all the animals to Adam and said, "Whatever you will call them, that will be their names." So Adam gave each one a name. God told Adam to take care of the garden and the animals.

Adam was happy, but God knew that Adam would soon be lonesome. There was no one else like him in the garden. The birds and the animals could not talk to him. They could only make sounds. The heavenly Father also knew that Adam needed a helper who would love him and would live with him.

So God made a woman and brought her to Adam. Adam was glad when he saw the woman. He called her Eve. Eve became Adam's wife. She was the first mother.

God made Adam and Eve without sin. At first they loved all that is good and nothing that is bad. They were good like God. The heavenly Father often came to see them and talked to them. He loved them and said He would give them many children.

The First Sin

Genesis 3:1-24

Adam and Eve, the first people, were very happy when they lived in the garden which God had given to them. They took care of the garden and the animals in it. God told them that they could enjoy the whole garden. But He said: "Do not eat of the fruit of that one tree which grows in the middle of the garden."

For a while Adam and Eve obeyed God. Then one day the devil came into the garden. The devil is a bad angel who tries to make people bad. He hid himself in a snake and made the snake talk. The devil came to Eve and said: "Did God really say, 'Don't eat the fruit of every tree in the garden'?" Eve answered: "God said that we must not eat of the fruit of that tree in the middle of the garden, or we will die." The devil said: "That's not true. When you eat that fruit, you will be like God."

When Eve heard this, she took some of the fruit and ate it. She also gave Adam some, and he ate it. Now Adam and Eve had disobeyed God, our Father in heaven. That was the first sin. Now Adam and Eve were no longer good. And they knew they had done wrong. At first they were ashamed, and then they became afraid. They tried to hide among the trees of the garden.

But God knew where Adam and Eve were and what they had done. Soon they heard God calling: "Adam, where are you?" When Adam answered, God asked: "Have you eaten some fruit from the tree of which I told you not to eat?" Adam said: "Eve gave me some, and I ate it." Eve said it was the devil's fault.

God was sorry that Adam and Eve had disobeyed Him. He would have to punish them as He had said He would. So God made Adam and Eve leave the pretty garden. He put angels in front of the garden and a big burning sword which kept them from going into it again. Now Adam and Eve were very unhappy.

But God still loved them, even though He had to punish them. He promised to send them a Savior. God said that the Savior would save them from the devil and from their sins.

How God Cared for Noah

Genesis 6:1 — 9:17

Adam and Eve were the first people God made. They had many children. When the children grew up, they had children, too. After a long time there were many, many people. But hardly any of the people loved God. Most people did not try to obey Him at all. They were so bad that God was sorry He had made them.

There was one man with whom God was pleased. His name was Noah. Noah and his family loved God and obeyed Him. One day God said to Noah, "I am going to send a big rain that will cover everything with water, but I will save you." Then He told Noah to build an ark. An ark is a big wooden boat built like a log house.

Noah obeyed the heavenly Father. He began building the ark. Many people must have laughed at him. When the ark was finished, God told Noah, "Go into the ark with your wife and children. Take with you two of every kind of bird and animal." He also told Noah to put lots of food in the ark. This was to feed his family and the birds and animals. Noah did all that God said he should do.

Then it began to rain. For many days and nights the rain came down. The water rose higher and higher. At last everything was covered with water. Outside the boat all the people drowned, but Noah and his family were safe inside the ark. No harm could come to them because God was taking care of them.

When the water went away, the ark landed on a mountain. As soon as the ground was dry, Noah opened the door of the ark. Then he and his family and all the birds and the animals hurried out. They were so glad that God had saved them.

The first thing Noah did was to show God how thankful he was. He piled up some stones and made an altar. Then he thanked the heavenly Father for taking care of him and his family.

God was pleased with what Noah did. He gave him a promise. He said, "I will never send such a big rain again." To remind people of His promise, God put a rainbow in the sky. Now, when we see a rainbow, we think of the big rain, and we remember God's promise to Noah.

The Boy Joseph

Genesis 37:1-36

Long ago there lived a boy named Joseph. Joseph's father, Jacob, had eleven other boys. Ten of them were older than Joseph, and one was younger. But Jacob loved Joseph most of all because Joseph was a good boy. He loved God and tried to obey Him.

When Joseph's brothers saw that their father loved Joseph more than he loved them, they didn't like Joseph. They said mean things about him.

One night Joseph had a dream. He told it to his brothers. This is what he said: "I dreamed that we were tying up bundles of grain in the field. All at once my bundle stood straight, and your bundles bowed down to my bundle." The brothers said: "Do you want to be a king over us? Do you think you are better than we are?"

Later Joseph had another dream. He told this dream too. He said: "In my dream I saw the sun and the moon and eleven stars bow to me." This made the brothers still more angry. They called him "the dreamer." When they would see Joseph walking by, they would make fun of him and say, "Here comes the dreamer."

Soon after this his brothers went far away from home with the sheep. They were gone a long time. One day Jacob called Joseph and said: "Go and see how your brothers are getting along, and come and tell me." Joseph obeyed his father right away.

When the brothers saw Joseph coming across the fields, they said, "Here comes the dreamer; let us kill him." "Oh, no," said the oldest brother. "Don't kill him. Let's just throw him into a deep empty well and leave him there."

So the brothers grabbed Joseph. They pulled off his pretty coat and threw him into a deep well. Joseph begged his brothers to take him out, but they just sat down and ate their lunch.

While they were eating, some peddlers came along. One of the brothers said: "Let's sell Joseph to these peddlers. They will take Joseph to a far-away country. Then we'll never be bothered with him again."

So they pulled Joseph out of the well and sold him. Joseph begged them not to, but they wouldn't listen. The peddlers took Joseph far away from home to a land called Egypt. But God went with Joseph.

God Takes Care of Joseph

Genesis 39:1 — 41:52

In Egypt Joseph had to work hard. Joseph's master saw that God helped Joseph in his work. So the master was kind to Joseph. He told him: "From now on I want you to take care of everything I have. I trust you."

But one day his master's wife asked him to do something wrong. Because Joseph loved God, he wouldn't do it. This made the woman angry. She told lies about Joseph. The master believed her and put Joseph into jail.

One night two other prisoners each had a dream. They told Joseph about their dreams, and God helped Joseph tell them what the dreams meant.

Later the king had a dream. When the king got up in the morning, he was worried. He called all of the wise men of Egypt to his palace and asked them what his dream meant. No one could tell him.

Then one of the men who had been in jail remembered Joseph. He said: "A young man in jail told me what my dream meant. What he said really happened." So the king said: "Hurry, and get Joseph." The king's helpers ran to get Joseph out of jail and brought him to the king.

When Joseph came, he bowed in front of the king. The king said: "I had a dream, but no one can tell me what it means. Someone told me that you can tell what a dream means." Joseph answered: "Not I. Only God knows the meaning of dreams. But He will give the king an answer that will help him."

So the king told Joseph his dream. He said: "In my dream I was standing by a river. Seven nice fat cows came out of it and began to eat grass by the river. Then seven thin cows came up out of the river and ate the seven fat cows."

Joseph said: "God has told the king what He is going to do. First there will be seven good years and plenty of food to eat in Egypt. Then there will be seven poor years. Very little food will grow, and people will eat up all the food and will still be hungry." Joseph also told the king to save some of the food while there was plenty. Then the people would have something to eat in the seven bad years.

The king was highly pleased with Joseph. He said: "Since God has told you all this, there is no one as wise as you." So he made Joseph the ruler over all his people.

Joseph Forgives His Brothers

Genesis 41:53 — 46:29

One day Joseph's father, Jacob, said to his sons: "I have heard that there is food in Egypt. Go down there and buy some so that we shall not starve." So Joseph's brothers had to go to Joseph in Egypt to buy food.

Joseph knew his brothers right away when he saw them, but they did not know him. He looked different now. The brothers all bowed down to him because he was a great man. Then Joseph remembered the dream God had given him long ago. Now it had come true. The brothers were bowing to Joseph.

At first Joseph didn't tell his brothers who he was. He was glad to see them, but he wanted to find out whether they were sorry for what they had done. So he talked roughly to them and put them into prison.

After three days he sent for them. "You may go home now," he said, "but the next time you come, you must bring your youngest brother. Otherwise you cannot buy food." Then Joseph's brothers became afraid. They remembered how they had sinned by selling Joseph. They were afraid God would punish them by taking their brother Benjamin away.

When the food was gone, the brothers came to Joseph again. He told his servant to fill their sacks. But he said to his servant: "Put my silver cup into the sack of the youngest brother."

The next morning the eleven brothers started for home. Soon Joseph's servant chased after them. He said, "One of you has stolen my master's cup." When they opened all the sacks, they found the cup in Benjamin's sack.

Now Benjamin had to go back to Joseph. The others all came back to help their brother. They would not leave him the way they had left Joseph. When Joseph saw that his brothers were no longer mean, he started to cry; he was so glad. He said: "I am Joseph. Is my father still living?"

At first the brothers were afraid. They thought Joseph would try to get even with them for what they had done to him long ago. But Joseph kissed them and forgave them.

The Story of Baby Moses

Exodus 1:1 — 2:10

Long ago there lived a father and a mother near a river. They had two children. One day God gave this family a beautiful baby boy. At that time there was a bad king in that country. He was trying to kill every baby boy who was born.

Now, the mother knew that the baby was a present from God. She did not want the king's soldiers to find her little boy. So she hid her baby in the house for a long time. Whenever he cried, she would quickly run and hush him up.

But the baby grew bigger and bigger. When it got harder and harder to hide him, the mother made a little basket. She rubbed tar all over it so that no water could get in. Then she laid her dear baby into the basket and carried him down to the river. There she hid him in the high grass along the side of the river.

The baby had a sister named Miriam. Miriam also loved the baby very much. She stood near the place where the baby had been put. She watched to make sure nothing would happen to her baby brother.

That very morning the king's daughter came down to the river. She was a princess. When the princess saw the basket in the high grass, she sent one of her maids to get it. They opened the basket. There lay the darling baby! Poor baby, he was crying! The princess felt so sorry for him. She wanted to keep him as her boy.

All of this time sister Miriam was watching and listening. She ran up to the princess and said, "Shall I go and get a nurse for the baby?" "Yes, do," said the princess. And whom do you think Miriam got? She hurried home and called her mother.

The princess didn't know that the woman was the baby's mother. She said, "Take the child home and nurse him for me; I will pay you." So the happy mother carried her baby home in her arms.

When the boy was old enough, the mother took him to the princess. "Here is your son," she said. The princess called him Moses. Now Moses lived in the king's palace and was a prince.

God took care of the baby Moses. He wanted Moses to grow up to be one of His helpers. He wanted Moses to help His people get away from the bad king. That is why God saved Moses.

How God Saved His People by the Sea

Exodus 13:7 — 15:21

When Moses became a man, God told him to take His people away from the bad king. For a long time the king would not let the people go. He wanted to keep them. He made them work hard for him. So God had to punish the king ten times. At last the king told the people to go, and Moses and the people were ready. As soon as the king said they could go, God's people started walking to a new home far away.

Pretty soon the king was sorry that he had let God's people go. He wanted them back to make bricks and build houses for him. So he called for his soldiers. "Take your horses and wagons," he said. "Chase after those people and bring them back here."

Pretty soon God's people came to a big lake of water called the Red Sea. Then they saw the soldiers coming after them with horses and wagons. They became very much afraid and prayed to God for help.

At first the people wanted to run away, but there was no bridge over the water. Around them were big hills. But Moses said to them: "Don't be afraid. God will fight for you." Then a big cloud came between God's people and the king's soldiers. Now the soldiers could not come near them.

Then God said to Moses: "Take your stick and hold it up over the sea." When Moses did this, God made a strong wind blow. All that night the wind blew the waters apart. That's how God made a road for His people right across the sea. The water stood up like a wall on both sides, and all the people walked over on dry ground.

In the morning the king and his soldiers wanted to cross the sea, too. They drove their horses and wagons down into the path. But when they were in the middle of the sea, God made their wagon wheels drop off. "Run away; God is helping these people," cried the soldiers. But God told Moses to hold out his stick again. Then the water came together. It covered the king and all of his soldiers.

When Moses and the people saw how God had helped them, they sang a song to praise God. "The Lord is my God," they said. "I will praise Him."

Why Ruth Helped Naomi

Ruth 1—4

For a long time there was no rain in the beautiful land where God's people lived long ago. Nothing would grow, and the people had very little to eat.

"We must go to another country until the heavenly Father sends rain," said a man to his wife, Naomi. So they took their two boys and everything they had and moved away. When the boys grew up, they married two young women. The one was called Orpah, the other Ruth.

Soon more troubles came to mother Naomi. First her husband died; then her two boys died. When she was all alone with Ruth and Orpah, she was very sad. She said to Ruth and Orpah, "I am going back to live with my own people in the place from which I came." But Ruth and Orpah would not let her go alone. They went along with her.

On the way Naomi stopped. "Go back home," she said. "May God be kind to you because you have been kind to me. Stay in your own country. I am sorry that all this trouble has come to you."

Then Orpah kissed Naomi good-bye and went back home. But Ruth loved Naomi very much. She would not leave her. She said, "Don't beg me to leave you or to stop following you. Your people will be my people, and your God will be my God." So the two women went to Naomi's home together.

When they came to Bethlehem, there was plenty of food again. Our heavenly Father had sent rain. The grain in the fields was ripe. But Ruth and Naomi were poor. They did not have anything to eat. They had no money to buy food. So God took care of them in another way.

In the morning Ruth went out into the fields and picked up some of the grain the workers let fall. In the evening she brought the grain to Naomi. From this they made bread.

The man who owned the field was a good man and he was rich. He spoke kindly to Ruth. He had heard how she helped Naomi. "Do not go to another field," he said to Ruth. "Stay in my field." The rich man loved her because she was a good woman. When all the grain was cut and put into barns, the rich man took Ruth to his home and married her.

Now Ruth didn't have to work in the fields anymore. She also took dear Naomi into her new home. Ruth knew that God had blessed her, and she was thankful. Later the Savior Jesus was born in her family.

A Boy Who Was Given to God

1 Samuel 1:1-28

Long, long ago there lived a good woman named Hannah. She had a husband whose name was Elkanah. Elkanah was kind to Hannah because he loved her. But often Hannah was very sad. She did not have any children. Oh, how she wished God would give her a little baby to love!

Often Hannah's husband found her crying. He would say to her, "Hannah, why do you cry? Am I not better to you than ten children would be?" Still she wanted a baby more than anything else.

One day Hannah went to God's house with her husband. God's house was the tent church in another town. In the church Hannah and Elkanah gave gifts to God and prayed and sang.

While Hannah was praying, she began to cry again. She was still wishing God would send her a little baby. She said to God: "Dear Father in heaven, if you will give me a baby boy, I will give him back to You, and he will be Your helper as long as he lives."

Hannah stayed in the church a long time that day. The priest, or minister, was sitting nearby. His name was Eli. He watched Hannah. He saw her lips moving, but he did not hear any words. So Eli spoke to Hannah. Hannah told him: "I am praying because my heart is very sad. I have talked to God about my trouble." Eli was a kind old priest. He said: "Go home. May God give you what you have prayed for."

The next morning Hannah and her husband went back home. They were happy now. They were sure that God would send them a baby. After a while God did answer Hannah's prayer. He gave her a dear little baby boy. She called him Samuel. Hannah loved Samuel and took very good care of him. Every day she also told him about God and taught him to pray to God.

When Samuel was still small, his mother took him to the big tent church. There she said to Eli, the priest: "I prayed for this child and God answered my prayer. Now he is to work for God as long as he lives."

Eli was glad to have a boy to help him in the church. So Samuel stayed with Eli in God's house and became a minister. It was hard for Hannah to leave her dear little boy. But every year she came to visit Samuel at the church. Whenever she came, she brought him a pretty new coat she had made.

When God Spoke to Samuel

1 Samuel 2:12—4:18

Samuel lived with Eli, the priest, in the big tent church. He was Eli's helper. He did many things for Eli, who was an old man. Samuel was glad to be a helper in his church.

Eli soon learned to love the little boy who was so willing to help him. Samuel's mother was glad, too, that Samuel was a good boy and a good helper in God's house. Every year she came to see him. Each time she brought him a new coat she had made for him.

Eli had two grown-up sons. They also helped in God's house. But they were not like Samuel. They did not love God, and they did many wicked things. They did not obey their father, and they often took things from the church. That is why God later chose Samuel to be His priest instead of Eli's sons.

At night Eli slept in a room in God's house, and Samuel slept in a little room near Eli. One night soon after Samuel and Eli had gone to bed, Samuel heard a voice calling to him, "Samuel!" He jumped up and ran to Eli. "Here am I," he said. He thought Eli was calling him. But Eli said: "I did not call you, my son; lie down again." So Samuel went back to his bed.

Soon Samuel heard a voice calling a second time, "Samuel!" He got up at once and ran to Eli. "Here am I," he said. He thought Eli was calling him. But Eli said: "I did not call you, my son; lie down again." So Samuel went back to his bed a second time. Then Samuel heard a voice calling a third time, "Samuel!" Again he ran to Eli. "Here am I, because you called me," he said.

Now Eli knew that the Lord God was calling Samuel. So Eli said to him: "Go and lie down. If you hear the voice calling you again, say: 'Speak, Lord; I am listening.'" So Samuel went back to his bed.

Soon he heard the voice calling, "Samuel! Samuel!" And he said: "Speak, Lord; I am listening." Then the Lord God spoke to Samuel and told him many things. He also told Samuel He was going to punish Eli and his sons because they were bad and because Eli did not try to stop them from being bad.

After that God talked with Samuel often. When Samuel grew up, he became a minister and a preacher. He taught God's Word to other people. He also became the leader of God's people.

Why God Chose David

1 Samuel 8:1 — 16:13

For a long time Samuel was the ruler of God's people. When Samuel was an old man, the people came to him and said, "Give us a king to rule over us." Samuel was not pleased with this. But he prayed to God, and God said, "You may give them a king if they want one."

Soon after this a man named Saul came to Samuel. Saul was a tall and strong man. God said to Samuel, "This is the man who is to be the king over My people."

Then Samuel called all the people to a meeting. He told Saul to stand up where everyone could see him. "This is the man God has chosen to be your king," he said. When the people saw what a fine-looking man Saul was, they shouted: "God save the king!"

Now at first Saul was a good king. But Saul did not stay good. Often he did not obey God. At last God said to Samuel, "I am sorry I have made Saul the king, for he has not done what I have commanded." So Samuel went and told Saul, "It is better to obey God than to give Him offerings. Because you did not obey God, you cannot be king any longer."

A little later God said to Samuel: "Go to the little town of Bethlehem and visit a man named Jesse, who lives there. I have chosen one of his sons to be the king." So Samuel did what God told him to do. He went to Bethlehem and asked to see Jesse's seven boys. First the oldest one came. When Samuel saw how tall and good-looking he was, he said to himself, "This must be the man God has chosen king." But God said to Samuel, "You must not choose a man because he is tall or good-looking. I have not chosen this one. The Lord looks at the heart."

Then the other brothers came to Samuel, one at a time. Each time Samuel said, "This is not the man God has chosen." At last Samuel said to the father, "Are these all of your children?" The father answered, "I have one other boy, the youngest. He is watching the sheep." "Send for him, and bring him to me," said Samuel. So the father sent someone out to the field to call David.

In a little while the man came back with David. David was not as tall as his brothers. But he was strong and had rosy cheeks and bright eyes. Samuel was pleased to see him. God said to Samuel, "Pour oil on his head, for he is the one I have chosen king." Then Samuel took a horn full of oil and poured it on David's head. In those days that was the way they showed who should be king. God chose David to be the king of His people because David loved God in his heart.

How God Helped David

1 Samuel 17

David was a shepherd boy. He took care of his father's sheep. His brothers were away from home. They were fighting in King Saul's army.

One day David's father called him and said: "Go and see how your brothers are. Take this bread to them, and take this cheese to their captain." David obeyed and took the food to his brothers.

While David was talking to his brothers, he heard a loud voice calling. "Come out and fight me," said the loud voice. David looked over to where the enemy soldiers were standing. There stood a great giant. The giant was shaking a big spear at King Saul's soldiers. He was laughing at them and saying bad words about them and about God.

"Won't anyone fight this giant?" asked David. No one would. All the soldiers were afraid. Even King Saul and David's big brothers were afraid. So David said, "I'll fight the giant. God will help me fight him."

At first King Saul thought David was too little to fight the giant. But after a while he said, "Go, and the Lord be with you."

Now, David had no sword and no spear like the giant. He didn't have a coat of iron either. He had only his shepherd's stick and a sling. But David wasn't afraid. He believed that God would help him fight the giant.

On the way out to meet the giant, David picked up five little stones and put them in his shepherd's bag. When the giant came out and saw that David was only a boy with a stick, he laughed and said: "Am I a dog that you come to me with a stick?" The giant made fun of David and of God, too.

But David answered: "God will help me fight against you." Then David took one of the little stones out of his bag and put it in his sling. He aimed at the giant and let the stone fly out of his sling. The stone hit the giant in the head, and he fell down and died.

When the enemy soldiers saw what had happened to their strong man, they all ran away. God had helped David save his people. They praised God for this.

Two Friends Who Loved Each Other

1 Samuel 18:1 — 20:42

King Saul had a son. His name was Jonathan. Jonathan loved God and was a good soldier. In the king's house lived another brave soldier. His name was David. David had killed the giant who had made fun of God's people. That is why the king had asked David to live in his palace.

Jonathan was a prince. He wore a fine coat and belt. He had a sword and a beautiful bow with arrows. David was a poor shepherd boy. He had no fine clothes. But Jonathan loved David very much because David loved God and was brave.

When David came to live in the palace, he and Jonathan made a promise. They promised always to be friends with each other. To show his love, Jonathan took off his fine coat and belt and gave them to David. He even gave David his sword and his bow and arrows.

King Saul made David a captain in his army. He also gave him some soldiers. David and his soldiers helped the king fight their enemies. Because God helped David, he won many battles.

Then Saul began to think that David would soon become the king. That made him hate David. The king even told Jonathan and his servants to kill David. But Jonathan loved David, so he went to David and said: "My father wants to hurt you. Go and hide. I will talk to my father."

Then Jonathan went back and talked to his father. He said: "Do not sin by trying to hurt David. Whatever he has done for you has been good." This made Saul sorry. He said, "I will not harm David." So Jonathan brought David back to live in the palace.

But soon Saul became angry again, so David had to run away and hide again. Jonathan visited him in his hiding place. "You must go far away," said Jonathan. "My father wants to hurt you."

David and Jonathan were very sad because they had to say good-bye. They kissed each other and cried. And as long as Jonathan lived, he loved David as his best friend.

A Little Girl Who Helped a Sick Man

2 Kings 5:1-27

Many years ago a little girl was stolen from her parents. Some soldiers carried her far away to another country. There she became a maid in a captain's home. His name was Naaman. The little girl helped Naaman's wife with her work.

The little girl remembered that our heavenly Father loved her and was with her. So she loved Him. When she was sad, she would pray, and God would make her happy again. Instead of hating the captain and his wife, she tried hard to help and please them.

Naaman and his wife lived in a big house, for he was a very rich man. He was also a dear friend of the king and a very great man. But Naaman and his wife were very sad because Naaman had leprosy. That was a very bad sickness. No doctor could help people with leprosy. It makes the skin look white like snow and full of ugly sores.

The little girl felt sorry for Naaman and his wife. She wanted to help her master get well. One day she said to Naaman's wife: "Oh, how I wish Naaman would go to the prophet in my country! He would cure my master of his sickness." When the king heard what the little girl had said, he called for Naaman. "You must go to the prophet and be healed," he said. So the captain went and took with him many servants and many, many presents.

When Naaman came to the prophet Elisha's house, the prophet did not even come out to talk with him. Elisha's servant came out and said: "Go and wash seven times in the Jordan River, and your skin will be new and clean." At first this made Naaman angry. He did not want to do what the prophet had said. He did not think that it would help him. So he started to go back home.

But Naaman's servants talked to him. They said: "If the prophet had asked you to do something hard, wouldn't you have done it? Then why don't you do what he said?" So Naaman went down to the Jordan River and put himself under the water seven times. After he had done this, he looked at himself. The white skin and the ugly sores were gone!

When Naaman saw that he was healed, he hurried back to thank the prophet. He said to Elisha: "Now I know that there is no God except Elisha's God." Then he begged Elisha to take some presents. But the prophet Elisha would not take any gifts. He wanted Naaman to thank God. Then Naaman said: "I will never again pray to any other gods."

Daniel and His Friends

Daniel 1:1-20

Once there were four young men who lived in a country where the people didn't know or love our Father in heaven. The king of that country told his servant: "I want these young men to go to school so they can learn how to help me rule my people. Give them the same rich food that I eat, so they will grow to be strong and healthy."

The servant told the men what the king had said they should do. But one of the men, whose name was Daniel, said: "We will go to the king's school, but please do not ask us to eat the king's food, because that food is given to idols. We want to obey and please God." The king's servant said: "If you don't eat the king's food, you will not grow strong and healthy. Then the king will become angry with me."

Daniel thought about what the servant said. He believed that God could make him strong even though he didn't eat the king's food. So when another servant brought some of the king's food to Daniel and his friends, Daniel said to him: "Please take this meat and red wine away. Let us eat vegetables and cereal and drink water instead. After ten days you will see whether we look stronger and healthier than the young men who eat the king's food."

The servant said he would try Daniel's plan. For ten days he brought them vegetables and cereal to eat and water to drink. For ten days he gave the other young men the food from the king's table. When the ten days were over, the servant could see that Daniel and his friends looked healthier than the young men who ate the king's food. Because they loved God and wanted to obey Him, God made them strong and healthy. So the servant said: "All right, you won't ever have to eat the king's food."

At the king's school Daniel and his friends studied hard. They learned to read and write the language of that country. God helped them to become very wise. When they had finished school, the king commanded that they should be brought in to see him. The other young men, who had eaten the food offered to idols, also were brought before the king.

The king talked with all the young men. He asked them what they had learned. Soon he saw that the wisest and the healthiest young men were Daniel and his friends—the young men whom God had blessed.

How Daniel Was Saved from Lions

Daniel 6:1-28

The king of the country where Daniel lived liked him because he was a wise and good man. He made Daniel one of the rulers of his country. But the king had many other princes and helpers. These men hated Daniel because the king loved and honored him more than anyone else. They watched Daniel to see whether he would do anything wrong. They were going to tell the king so that he would punish Daniel.

But Daniel did his work faithfully. They could not find anything wrong to tell. But they did notice that Daniel prayed to God by a window in his house every day. So Daniel's enemies went to the king. They said to him: "All of your helpers want you to make this rule: Whoever will pray to any god except the king, he will be put into the den of lions." The king did not know why the men wanted the rule, but he made it.

Then Daniel's enemies hurried over to his house to catch him praying. Daniel knew about the rule, but still he prayed to God by the window as before. When his enemies saw him praying, they hurried to tell the king.

"Didn't you make a rule that anyone who would pray to any god except the king should be put into the den of lions?" they asked. "Yes," said the king. "That's the rule." "But Daniel is not obeying you," said his enemies.

Now the king wished he had not made the rule. All day long he tried to think of a way to save Daniel. But the enemies said: "Daniel must be put into the lions' den because he did not obey the king's rule." The king was very, very sorry, but he told his men to take Daniel to the lions' den. "Your God will save you," the king said to Daniel.

But the king was very sad. He would not eat his supper or listen to music. He was so worried about Daniel that he could not sleep all that night. Early the next morning he hurried to the lions' den to see if Daniel was still alive. "O Daniel," he called, "did your God save you from the lions?"

Daniel answered: "My God sent His angel and shut the lions' mouths. They could not hurt me." Oh, how glad the king was! He told his men to get Daniel out of the lions' den at once.

When Daniel came out, the king saw that the lions had not hurt Daniel at all. God had taken care of him because he had trusted in God. Then the king told the people that Daniel's God was the true God and that all the people should pray to Daniel's God. The king also made Daniel his main helper.

A Man Who Ran Away from God

The Book of Jonah

Jonah was a prophet—one of God's helpers. One day God told Jonah: "Go to the city of Nineveh. Tell the people that they are doing wrong and that I will punish them."

Jonah didn't want to obey God. He tried to run away from God. He got on a boat that was going far away. But God knew Jonah was on the boat that was sailing over the ocean. So God sent a big storm over the water. The sky grew dark. The wind roared. Big waves splashed over the boat. The people on the boat became very frightened.

"Why is God sending this storm?" they asked. When Jonah told them how he had not minded God, they asked him, "What shall we do?" "Throw me into the ocean," Jonah told them. "Then God will stop the storm."

So the people on the boat threw Jonah into the water. At once the storm stopped. Then God sent a big fish that swallowed Jonah in the water. For three days and three nights Jonah was inside the fish. Jonah prayed to God inside the fish, for now he was sorry that he hadn't minded God.

God heard Jonah's prayer from inside the fish and forgave him. Then God told the fish to spit Jonah up on the dry land. After that happened, God told Jonah again: "Go to Nineveh, and preach to the people."

This time Jonah went. When he got to the city, he preached to the people in the streets. "Because you are so wicked, God will destroy this city," he told them.

The people of Nineveh listened to Jonah. They believed God. They all began to pray to God. "Please, God, forgive us what we have done wrong," they prayed.

And our Father in heaven heard their prayer, too. He felt sorry for the people. He forgave them their many sins. He did not destroy the city.

The First Christmas

Luke 2:1-7

Joseph and Mary lived together in a little home in Nazareth. They were poor, but they were very happy. An angel had said, "Mary, you will be the mother of a wonderful baby. He will be God's Son."

The angel had also come to Joseph and said, "When God gives Mary her dear little baby, you are to call Him Jesus, for He will save His people from their sins." So Joseph had asked Mary to live with him. Mary was Joseph's wife.

One day Joseph and Mary had to go away from their home in Nazareth. A great king wanted to find out how many people there were in his lands. He said all the people should be counted. Everyone was to go to the place where his father and mother had lived.

So Mary and Joseph had to go to the little town of Bethlehem to be counted. It was a long, long way. It took them at least four days to go that far. When they came to Bethlehem, they were both very tired. They wanted to lie down and sleep in a warm bed.

But many other people had come to Bethlehem to write their names in the king's book. All the houses were filled with visitors. Joseph and Mary could find no place to stay. They knocked on many doors, but the people said, "We have no room." The big house where people stayed overnight was also filled. It was called an inn.

Where could Mary and Joseph go? Mary was very tired. She must have a place to sleep. Behind the inn was a stable where the animals were kept. Some sheep and cows were in there, but it was dry and warm. Joseph led his little donkey into the stable and helped Mary make a soft bed out of hay. There in the stable they lay down to rest.

That night something wonderful happened. The Baby Jesus was born. The heavenly Father gave the Baby Jesus to Mary, just as He had promised. Mary had no soft bed for the Baby, but there was a manger, a box from which the animals ate their hay. So Mary wrapped the dear little Baby Jesus in some cloth. Then she made a warm little bed of hay in the manger and laid the Baby in it.

And do you know? This little Baby Jesus was God's own Son. Our Father in heaven had sent Him to save all people from their sins. Wasn't that a wonderful Christmas Gift from God?

The Song of Christmas Angels

Luke 2:8-20

On the night when Jesus was born, some shepherds were in the fields near the little town of Bethlehem. They were taking care of their sheep. The night was dark, but all at once a wonderful light came down from heaven. It was brighter than the sun, and it was shining all around them. An angel sent by God was in the light.

At first the shepherds were very much afraid. But the angel said: "Don't be afraid. I bring you good news, which is for all people. The Savior was born this night in Bethlehem. You will find Him lying in a manger."

Then the shepherds saw many, many angels there above the fields in Bethlehem. The angels had come from heaven to praise God for sending His Son Jesus. They were glad He would be the Savior of all people. They sang: "Glory to God in the highest, and on earth peace, goodwill toward men." After that the angels went back to heaven and it was dark again.

For a while the shepherds were very quiet. They were wondering about the wonderful thing they had seen. They were thinking about the good news they had heard from the angels. Then they said: "Let us go to Bethlehem and see the Savior."

So the shepherds left their sheep and hurried off to Bethlehem. There they found Mary and Joseph in the stable and the Baby Jesus lying in His manger bed. How happy the shepherds were! They knew that this Baby was God's own Son. They knew He had come to save them and all people from their sins.

The shepherds were thankful. They got down on their knees and prayed to the Baby Jesus. Then they told Mary and Joseph what the angel had said and how the angels had sung praises to God. Mary and Joseph listened to the shepherds, and Mary kept on thinking about everything they had told her. Just think! Her Baby Jesus was God's Son! He was the Savior God had promised to send!

When the shepherds went back home, what do you think they did? They told everybody that the Savior had come. Like the angels, they were happy and thankful. They praised God for sending the Savior.

When Baby Jesus Was Brought to the Temple

Luke 2:21-38

Mary and Joseph gave the name Jesus to their Baby. It was the name which the angel had told them to give to Him. Jesus means Savior.

When Jesus was still a wee baby, His father and mother took Him to the temple-church in the big city of Jerusalem. A long time ago God had said that all fathers and mothers should bring their little babies to the church. This would show that the baby belonged to God.

Mary and Joseph wanted to obey God. They also wanted to bring God a present. Long ago God had asked parents to do that, too.

Many other people came to the temple at Jerusalem. They came to pray and to give presents to God. A good man named Simeon was there. Simeon loved God. He knew that God had promised to send a Savior. He had waited a long time for the Savior to come.

God knew how Simeon felt. One day He said to Simeon: "You will not die until you have seen the Savior." This promise made Simeon glad. He was sure that the Savior would come soon.

When Simeon saw the Baby Jesus in God's house, he knew that the Savior had come. God had whispered to him: "This is the Savior. He has come to save all people from their sins." So he took the little Child and held Him in his arms. He was so happy.

Then Simeon thanked God for letting him see the Savior. He thanked God for sending the Savior. He said: "Lord, now I am ready to die, for I have seen the Savior, whom You have sent for all people."

While Simeon was speaking, an old lady came in. Her name was Anna. When Anna saw the Baby Jesus, she also knew that He was the Savior. First she, too, thanked God for sending His Son. Then she said to the people who were listening: "You can be happy now. The heavenly Father has sent the Baby Jesus to help you and to save you from your sins."

Gifts for Our Lord Jesus

Matthew 2:1-12

In a country far away from where Jesus was born, there lived some Wise Men who studied the stars. One night they saw a bright new star shining in the sky. It was the brightest star they had ever seen. "This star shows that God's Son has come to earth," they said. "Let us go and see Him. He is our King and Savior."

So they sent for their camels and got ready to go. "We must take Him some gifts to show that we love Him," said the Wise Men. "Let us take Him gifts lovely enough for a King."

So into their bags they put gold and sweet-smelling perfume. Then they started on a long trip to see the newborn King.

On and on they went until they came to a big city. It was called Jerusalem. There they asked: "Where is the Baby who is born to be a King? We have seen His star and have come to worship Him."

None of the people had heard of the Baby Jesus, but someone went and told the king who lived in the palace. This king's name was Herod.

When Herod heard that another king was born, he sent for the strangers and asked them about the star. Then he called some of his ministers who read the Bible. He asked them, "Where is the Savior to be born?" They told him, "The Bible says the Savior will be born in the city of Bethlehem."

So the Wise Men climbed up on their camels and started off for Bethlehem. It was nighttime as they rode away. All at once they saw the bright star shining again in the sky. How glad they were, for they knew God had sent the star to lead them to the Savior.

The star went ahead of them. At last it stood still above the house where the Baby Jesus was. When the Wise Men went in, they found Mary and Joseph and the Baby Jesus in the house.

The Wise Men bowed down on their knees and thanked Jesus for coming to help them. They knew He was their King and Savior. Then they opened their bags and gave Him the gifts which they had brought. The next day they went back to their home very happy.

Baby Jesus and the Bad King

Matthew 2:13-15, 19-23

The night was cold and dark in the little town of Bethlehem. But inside Jesus' house it was warm and quiet. Mary and Joseph and Baby Jesus were sleeping. And while they slept, our heavenly Father was watching over them.

That night the heavenly Father sent an angel to talk to Joseph in a dream. "Get up," the angel said to Joseph; "take Jesus and His mother far away from Bethlehem, and don't come back until I tell you. There is a bad king who wants to hurt Jesus."

When Joseph awoke, he did just what the angel had told him to do. He woke Mary, and that very night they got ready to leave. Mary wrapped the Baby in warm blankets and held Him close to herself. Joseph got their donkey ready and lifted Mary up on it.

Then out into the dark and cold night they went. It would be a long trip for such a little baby. But Mary and Joseph weren't afraid. They knew God would take care of them on the way.

Far away to a land called Egypt they went. There they all were safe from the bad king. When the king's soldiers came to Bethlehem, they could not hurt the Baby Jesus. They could not find Him.

When Jesus was a little older, God sent an angel to Joseph again. "Come back home," said the angel; "the bad king is dead."

Then Joseph and Mary took Jesus to their home in Nazareth. Here, too, God took care of them, just as He had done in Bethlehem and in Egypt. Baby Jesus grew and grew the way God wanted Him to grow. Pretty soon He was big enough to go to school.

The Boy Jesus in God's House

Luke 2:41-52

Jesus grew up in the little town of Nazareth. When He was small, Joseph and Mary told Him about the heavenly Father. They also taught Him to pray. As soon as He was old enough, He went to school. There He learned God's Word, just as you do.

Every year Joseph and Mary went to the big city of Jerusalem. They went to worship in a very beautiful church. It was called the temple. People from many places came to this special house of God.

When Jesus was twelve years old, Joseph and Mary took Him along with them to the temple. Early one morning they started off for Jerusalem, together with many other people. How happy Jesus was! They were all going to the big church together.

They walked many days. At last they came to the big city. Everybody shouted when they saw the beautiful church on top of a hill. They were happy. The next day Jesus went with His parents to the temple to pray and to hear God's Word.

When the church services were over, the people of Nazareth started to go home. Joseph and Mary started back, too. But Jesus was not with them. At first His parents did not worry. They thought Jesus was with some of their friends in the crowd.

But that evening Mary and Joseph looked for Jesus and could not find Him. They asked many people, "Did you see Jesus? Did you see Jesus?" But no one had seen Him. Mary and Joseph were so worried they could not sleep that night.

The next morning they went all the way back to Jerusalem and hunted for Jesus in the city. For three days they hunted. At last they found Jesus in the temple. He was sitting with the teachers and asking and answering questions about God's Word.

Mary ran up to Him and said: "My Son, why did You do this? We have been looking all over for You for three days." Jesus said: "Didn't you know that I must be doing My Father's work?" His heavenly Father had sent Him to save people from their sins, and He was already doing that.

Jesus loved His heavenly Father's house. He was happy when He could talk about God's Word. He wanted to stay in the temple longer, but He loved His parents and always obeyed them. So He went home with Joseph and Mary and gladly did whatever they asked Him to do.

The Baptism of Jesus

Matthew 3:1-17; John 1:19-34

John was a cousin of Jesus. He was born about the same time Jesus was. When John was grown up, God said to him one day: "Go and preach to people." So John began preaching near the River Jordan.

Many people came to listen to John. "The Savior will soon be here," he told them. "You must be sorry for your sins and begin to do what is right, otherwise you cannot have Jesus as your Savior and King," he said.

Some of the people told John that they had done wrong. They were glad that Jesus the Savior was coming to take away their sins. John baptized the people who were sorry for their sins and wanted Jesus to be their Savior. That is why he is called John the Baptizer. When he put the water on the people, God washed away their sins.

One day Jesus came to John to be baptized. Jesus was a grown-up man now. John was surprised that Jesus wanted to be baptized. He said to Jesus, "I need to be baptized by You." John knew that Jesus was God's Son. He knew that Jesus had never done anything wrong.

But Jesus said to John, "You must do as I say, for I want to do everything My heavenly Father wants people to do." When John heard this, he obeyed Jesus and baptized Him.

After His baptism, Jesus came up out of the river and prayed to the heavenly Father. Then something wonderful happened. The sky opened up, and a dove came down to Jesus and sat on Him. Then the voice of the heavenly Father said: "This is My beloved Son, in whom I am well pleased."

When John heard these words, he was glad. Now all who saw what happened knew that John had told the truth. The Son of God had come to be everybody's Savior.

When John saw Jesus a little later, he pointed to Jesus and said: "See, there is the Lamb of God, who takes away the sin of the world."

When Jesus Went to a Wedding

John 2:1-11

One time Jesus and His friends were invited to a wedding. Mary, the mother of Jesus, was there too. Many other people also came to the wedding. There were so many people that there wasn't enough wine for all of them.

Mary saw that the wine was all gone. She felt sorry for her friends who had invited the people. She couldn't help, but she thought of Jesus. "Jesus can help," she said to herself. So she went to Jesus and told Him the trouble. "They have no wine to drink," she said. Her words were a prayer. She was asking Jesus to help.

Jesus answered: "Why do you worry about that? The right time has not yet come for Me to help." But Mary knew that Jesus would help as soon as He was ready. So she went to the servants and said: "Whatever He says to you, do it."

By the door stood six big pots. They were used for keeping water. After a while Jesus said to the servants: "Fill the water pots with water."

The servants obeyed. They filled the pots with water up to the top. Then something wonderful happened. Without saying a word, Jesus changed the water into wine.

Jesus said to the servants: "Pour some out, and bring it to the man taking care of the meal." When the man taking care of the meal tasted the wine, he was surprised. It tasted much better than the wine they had before.

The man taking care of the meal called the young man who was just married and said: "People always give the good wine first to their company, but you have kept the good wine until now." Then the servants told him what had happened. Jesus had changed the water into wine.

This was the first time that Jesus, the Son of God, did what no other man could do. Such a work is called a miracle. By doing this miracle Jesus showed that He is the Son of God. He had come to save all people—and to help them also in their work and play.

The First Helpers of Jesus

Luke 5:1-11

In the land where Jesus lived there is a beautiful lake of water. It is called the Sea of Galilee. One day Jesus was preaching near this water. A big crowd came to listen to Him. The people pushed close to Jesus to hear Him.

Near the shore were two little boats. Jesus stepped into one of them. It belonged to Peter, a friend of Jesus. Jesus said to Peter: "Take your ship out a little way from the land." Then Jesus sat down and taught the people out of the boat.

When Jesus finished preaching, He said to Peter: "Take your boat out to the deep water, and let down your nets for some fish." Peter said: "We worked all night and caught nothing. But because You say so, I will let down the net." So Peter and his friends rowed out to the deep water.

As soon as Peter and his helpers dropped the nets into the deep water, the nets became filled with fish. There were so many that the nets began to tear.

Peter and his helpers called to their friends in another boat to come and help them. They came and filled both of the ships with fish. The boats were so full that they began to sink.

When Peter saw what Jesus had done for them, He knew that Jesus really was God. Then Peter became afraid. He fell down on his knees in front of Jesus and said: "Go away from me, because I am a sinful man, O Lord."

But Jesus said to Peter: "Don't be afraid. From now on you shall catch men." He meant that Peter and the others were to tell people about Jesus, their Savior.

So when they had brought their boats to land, they left everything and followed Jesus.

The Lame Man Who Had No Friend

John 5:1-14

It was a holiday in the city of Jerusalem—a day for resting and for visiting friends. Many people said, "Let's go to the pool of Bethesda and visit our friends who are sick."

Jesus also went to the pool. When He got there, He saw a big crowd of sick people and visitors. Some of the sick people were blind. Others were lame and crippled. Some were so sick that they couldn't even move. All of them stayed close to the pool. They believed that if they could get into the water when it bubbled, then they would get well.

At the pool Jesus saw a sick man who had no other company. The man had been sick for a long, long time. Besides, he didn't have any friends or brothers or sisters who could help him into the water when it bubbled. All he could do was lie there on his blanket, day after day, wishing that someone would help him.

Worst of all, the man felt bad when he thought of the many wrong things he had done before he got sick. Maybe he thought God was punishing him. Jesus stopped and talked to the man. "Do you want to get well?" Jesus asked him.

"Sir, how *can* I get well?" the man answered. "I don't have any friends to help me into the pool. And when the water starts to bubble, somebody else always gets ahead of me."

Jesus looked at the man and said with a strong voice: "Get up, pick up your blanket, and walk."

As soon as Jesus said this, the man's sick body became well. He felt strong all over. Up from the ground he jumped. And, picking up his blanket, he began to walk. He could hardly believe what had happened!

Later on, Jesus saw the man again. "Now that you are well," Jesus said to him, "don't do bad things again. Use your healthy body to thank God and to be kind to other people."

The man was glad to be well. He was happy that Jesus was his Friend. From then on he wanted to do only good things.

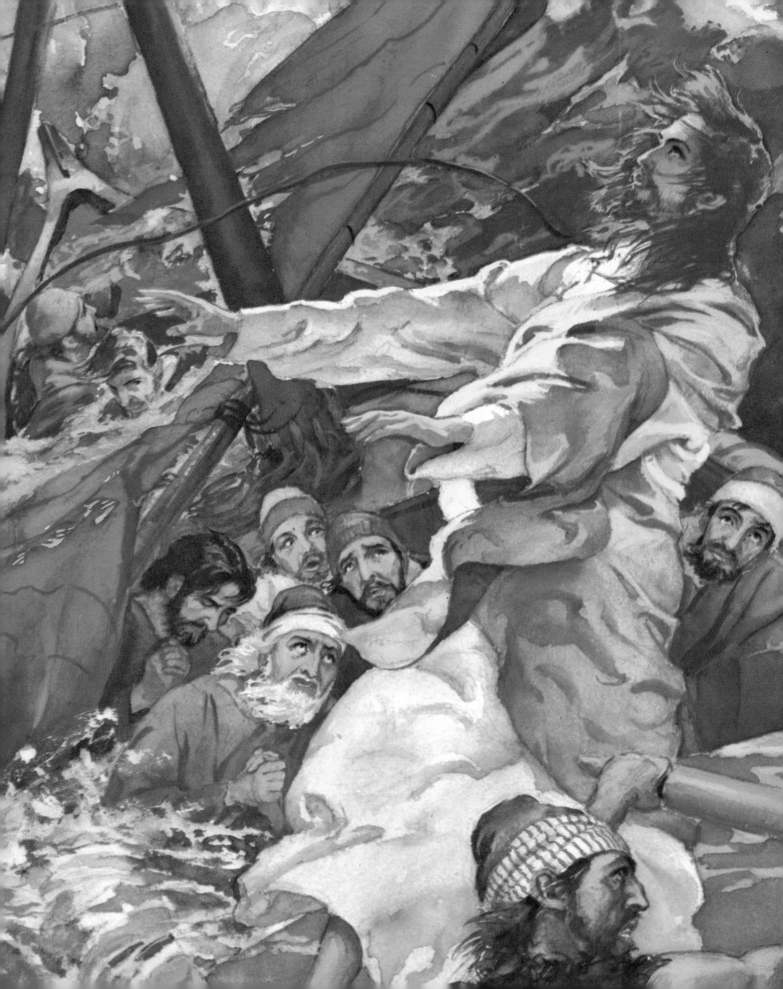

How Jesus Stopped a Storm

Matthew 8:23-27; Mark 4:35-41

One time Jesus had been working hard all day. He had been teaching and making sick people well. When evening came, He was very tired. He wanted to go somewhere and rest for a while with His helpers. So He sent the people away and stepped into a ship. He said to His disciples: "Let's go over to the other side of the lake."

The disciples rowed the boat out into the lake. As they sailed away, Jesus lay down in the back part of the ship. Soon He went to sleep.

While they were crossing the lake, a strong wind started blowing. The waves came into the ship and began to fill it with water. The disciples became very much afraid. They thought they would all be drowned.

So they awoke Jesus. "Lord, save us!" they cried. One of them said: "Master, Master, don't You care that we are drowning?"

Jesus looked up at them and said: "Why are you afraid? You have so little faith." If they had had more faith in Jesus, they would not have been so afraid. They would have expected Jesus to take care of them in any kind of trouble or danger.

Then Jesus arose and spoke to the wind and the water. He said: "Peace, be still!" Right away the wind stopped blowing, and the stormy waves became very still.

The disciples were surprised. They had found out something more about Jesus. They knew He could heal the sick, but they hadn't known He could quiet a storm, too. They thought, "What kind of man is this? Even the winds and the sea obey Him."

Now they were sure that Jesus was not just a man, but the Son of God. And they knew that nothing could harm them if they were friends of Jesus and He was with them.

A Man Who Couldn't Walk

Mark 2:1-12; Luke 5:17-26

It was a happy day in the city of Capernaum. All the people were very excited. "Jesus has come to visit us! Let's go see Him," said the people to one another.

Soon the house where Jesus was staying was filled with people. Even the enemies of Jesus were there. Boys and girls who had heard about Jesus were there, too. Jesus healed the sick people who were brought to Him. He also told the people, "I will help you become God's children."

While Jesus was talking, someone whispered, "Look!" Four men were coming down the street. They were carrying a man on a mattress. This man could not walk. He had been very, very sick for a long time. His friends knew that Jesus could help him; so they were bringing him to Jesus.

But when they came to the house, they couldn't get in. It was too crowded. "We must find a way to bring our friend to Jesus," they said. "Jesus can make him well." So up the stairs they went to the flat roof of the house. There they took away part of the roof. Then they tied ropes around the sick man's bed and let him down right in front of Jesus.

When Jesus saw what the friends had done, He said to the sick man: "Be happy; I forgive you your sins." The kind words of Jesus made the man glad. He had been afraid that Jesus wouldn't love him. When the enemies of Jesus heard what Jesus said, they began saying to themselves: "Only God can forgive sins."

Jesus knew what His enemies were thinking. "Why do you have bad thoughts in your hearts?" He asked. "Which is easier to say, 'Your sins are forgiven,' or 'Rise up and walk'? Now I will show you that I am the Son of God and that I have the right to forgive sins." Then Jesus turned to the sick man lying on his bed and said: "Get up, take your bed, and go."

Right away the sick man became strong and well. He stood up, took his bed, and carried it out of the house. When the enemies of Jesus saw what He had done, they hated Him more than ever. But all the other people were very glad. They praised God. They said: "We have never seen anything like this!"

How Jesus Made a Little Girl Alive

Luke 8:41-56

In the country where Jesus lived, there was a man named Jairus. He had a little daughter. She was his only child, and he loved her very much. One day she became very sick. Her mother and her father were afraid she would die. Nothing seemed to help her. Then the father thought of Jesus and hurried away to find Him.

When Jairus came to the place where Jesus was teaching, he pushed through the crowd and knelt in front of Jesus. "Lord, my little girl is very sick!" he said. "She is dying! Please come and put your hands on her so that she will get well."

Jesus went with Jairus right away, and a lot of people followed them. As they walked along the street, some men came up to them. They had bad news for the father. "Your little girl is dead," they said. "Don't bother Jesus anymore."

Jesus heard the bad news. He knew how sad the poor father was. He wanted Jairus to keep on trusting Him. So He said to Jairus: "Do not be afraid; only believe, and your girl will be made well."

When they came near the house, they heard a loud noise. Friends and neighbors were there. They were crying loudly because the little girl was dead.

"Why are you making so much noise and crying?" asked Jesus. "The little girl is not dead; she is only sleeping." Jesus meant that He could wake her up just as if she were asleep. He could make her alive again. But the people laughed at Him, because they knew that the little girl was dead.

Then Jesus told everyone to go out of the room, except three of His friends and the little girl's father and mother. Then He took hold of the girl's hand and said: "Little girl, I say, awake!" As soon as He spoke these words, the girl became alive again. She opened her eyes, got up, and walked around.

Her mother and father were so happy they didn't know what to say or do. Jesus had to tell them to give the girl something to eat. Now the parents knew that Jesus could even make dead people alive again. Those who knew this told many others.

When Jesus Fed Many People

Matthew 14:14-21; John 6:1-15

One day when Jesus was very tired, He said to His friends: "Let us go away to a quiet place and rest a while." So they got into a ship and crossed a big lake. But some of the people saw Jesus and His friends go away in the ship. So they began to walk around the lake. Many other people came out of their houses and went with them. They even brought sick persons to be healed.

When Jesus and His friends came to the other side of the lake, a big crowd was waiting for them. Jesus felt sorry for these people, who had walked a long way to hear God's Word. He told them about the heavenly Father's love and healed many sick persons. All day long the people were with Jesus on a big hill.

After a while it was time to eat. The people were far away from home. Jesus said to His helpers: "Where shall we buy bread so that all these people may eat?" He wanted to see if they would ask Him for food.

One of the men said: "There is a boy here who brought a lunch. He has five loaves of bread and two little fishes; but that is very little for so many people." Jesus answered: "Tell the people to sit down." So the helpers of Jesus told the people to sit down on the grass.

Then Jesus asked for the five loaves of bread and the two fish. The boy gladly gave his lunch to Jesus. Jesus took the bread and fish and thanked His heavenly Father for the food.

After that, something very wonderful happened. Jesus passed out the bread and fish, and made it enough food for all those many, many people. His helpers served it.

When the people were finished eating, there was even some food left. Jesus said to His helpers: "Pick up all the pieces which are left, so that nothing will be wasted." So they picked up twelve baskets full of food. That was much more than they had had at the beginning.

When the people saw what Jesus had done, they said: "This certainly is the Savior who was supposed to come."

God gives us our daily bread. So we ought to ask Him every day to give us something to eat. And every day we must thank Him for all the good foods He gives us.

When Jesus Walked on Water

Matthew 14:22-33; Mark 6:45-51; John 6:15-21

Jesus' helpers were in a boat far out on a lake. A big wind started blowing. It made the waves roll higher and higher. It made the boat rock up and down, up and down. Then it got so dark they couldn't see.

Jesus' helpers were all afraid. "We'll drown," they thought. "Row the boat harder!" they shouted. They rowed and rowed, but the big waves kept them back. The water kept splashing into the boat and almost tipped them over.

All through the dark night they rowed in the storm. As it began to get light again, they saw something moving over the water. It was coming toward them! Now they were terribly afraid. "It's a ghost!" they screamed.

But it was Jesus coming to help them. He was walking right on the water. "It's all right," Jesus called to them. "It is I. Don't be afraid."

When Peter saw it was Jesus, he became brave. He said: "Lord, if it's You, tell me to come to You on the water." Jesus said: "Come on."

So Peter *did* come. He knew he could do it because Jesus told him to come. Right on top of the water he walked. But then Peter began to look at the waves. How high they were! He listened to the wind. How hard it was blowing! And then Peter thought, "Can Jesus *really* keep me from sinking?" And when he thought that, down into the cold, deep water he started to go.

"Lord, save me!" Peter called as he began to sink. Right away Jesus reached out His hand. He pulled Peter up. "Why didn't you believe what I said? I told you you could walk on the water," He said to Peter.

Then Jesus and Peter walked to the boat and climbed in. As soon as they were in the boat, Jesus made the wind stop blowing. He made the waves go down. He stopped the storm.

What do you think His helpers did after they saw all this happen? They fell on their knees and said to Jesus: "You are truly the Son of God."

The Little Man Called Zacchaeus

Luke 19:1-10

One day Jesus and His friends came to a city called Jericho. A man named Zacchaeus lived there. The people didn't like this man Zacchaeus because he collected taxes. Sometimes he made the people pay too much. They said he was very bad.

Zacchaeus was a rich man. He lived in a beautiful house. But he was sad and lonely. He was sad because he knew he had done wrong.

When the people of Jericho heard that Jesus had come to their city, they hurried out of their houses to see Him. Soon there was a big crowd on the streets.

Zacchaeus wanted to see Jesus, too. But he was such a little man. He could not see over the heads of the other people. And the people around Jesus would not let Zacchaeus get close.

"I *must* see Jesus!" said Zacchaeus to himself. So he ran ahead of the crowd and climbed a tree. There he sat, waiting for Jesus to pass by that way.

When Jesus came to the place below the tree, He stopped and looked up. There was Zacchaeus, looking down. Jesus called to him. "Zacchaeus," He said, "come down quickly! Today I must stay at your house."

Zacchaeus was so surprised! He didn't think Jesus would love him. So he came down from the tree as fast as he could and gladly took Jesus to his home. The people who saw this became angry. They said, "Look, Jesus went to the home of a bad man!" But Jesus had done this on purpose. He wanted to show that He is the Friend of bad people, too, when they are sorry for their sins.

When they were in the house, Zacchaeus told Jesus he was sorry for the bad things he had done. He made a promise to Jesus. He said: "I will give half of all my money to the poor people. If I have taken too much money from any person, I will pay him back more than I took from him."

Jesus spoke kindly to Zacchaeus. He forgave him all his sins. Jesus is the Friend of sinners. He came to save us all. He said: "I have come to save that which was lost." Jesus is *our* Friend and Savior, too.

A Story About a Kind Man

Luke 10:25-37

Jesus often told stories which teach us how to love other people the way God loves us. One time He told this story:

A man was going on a trip from one city to another. The road went around big rocks and over hills. On the way some robbers jumped out at this man and caught him. They hit him with clubs. They took his money and everything he had with him. They even tore off his clothes and left him lying on the road almost dead.

By and by a man from the church came down the road. He saw the one who was hurt, but he did not stop to help him. He walked right on by. Soon after this another man came walking along the road. Maybe he would help the poor man who was hurt. But no; he looked at the hurt man and then hurried away.

After a while a man came along the road on a donkey. He was from a different country. But when this stranger saw the man who needed help, he felt sorry for him. He went to him, put some medicine on his cuts and sores, and tied some cloth over them. Then he carefully lifted the man up and put him on the back of the donkey.

By and by they came to an inn. An inn was a big house or hotel, where people who were on a trip could stay. The stranger carried the hurt man into the house. He put him to bed and took care of him all night. The next morning the stranger had to leave. But he gave the owner of the house some money and said: "Take care of the man. If you need more money, I will pay you the next time I come."

Jesus told this story to show that our Father in heaven wants His children to be kind. When He had finished the story, Jesus asked: "Which of the three men acted like a good neighbor to the man who was hurt by the robbers?" Someone answered: "The man who helped." Jesus said: "Go and do as he did."

Jesus and the Children

Mark 10:13-16

Some people think that children are too small to go to church in order to learn about Jesus. But Jesus wants even the small children to come to Him. He loves children and wants them all in His church.

One day Jesus came to a place and was talking to people about His church. Everybody wanted to see Him and came to listen to Him. He helped the sick and told people how they could be God's children. Soon a big crowd was around Him.

Some mothers wanted Jesus to help their children, too. So they said: "Let's go to see Jesus. Let's ask Jesus to love and teach our little children and bless them."

The mothers hurried and got their children ready. Oh, how excited they all were! They thought of how happy they would be if Jesus would speak to them and would touch them.

But when the mothers came to Jesus with their children, some of His friends stopped them. They said: "Go away. Jesus is too busy. He doesn't want children to bother Him."

When Jesus saw what His friends had said and done, He was very angry. He didn't want children kept away from Him. He said: "Let the little children come to Me, and forbid them not."

Then He called the children to Him. He took the babies into His arms. He put His hands on the heads of the little boys and girls. In this way He showed that He loved them.

Jesus loves all little children. He wants them in His church. We love Jesus because He is our Friend and Savior. He came to save us from our sins so that we could all be God's children.

A Loving Gift for Jesus

Matthew 26:6-13; John 12:1-8

One day Jesus came to the little town of Bethany. Mary and Martha and Lazarus lived in Bethany. They were friends of Jesus. Other friends of Jesus lived there, too. One of them was called Simon. Simon loved Jesus because Jesus had taken away his sickness.

The friends of Jesus wanted to show Him how much they loved Him. Simon said he would make a supper and invite Jesus and His helpers. Martha wanted to show her love for Jesus; so she went to Simon's house to help get the supper ready. Mary did not tell what she was going to do. She wanted to give Jesus something special.

When Jesus and His helpers came to Simon's house, they all sat around the supper table. Martha helped bring in the food and saw to it that everyone had enough to eat.

While the men were eating, Mary came quietly up to Jesus. She carried a pretty little jar which had very expensive perfume in it. It cost a lot of money, and it smelled very sweet. It was the best gift she could give. "I must show Jesus how much I love Him!" she thought. So she opened the jar and poured some of the perfume on Jesus' head. The rest she poured on His feet. Then she knelt down and wiped His feet with her beautiful long hair.

As soon as the jar was opened, everyone noticed the sweet smell. When they saw what she had done, some of the men got angry. They thought Mary had wasted the rich perfume. Some of them said: "Why was this expensive perfume wasted?" A disciple whose name was Judas said: "This perfume cost a lot of money. It should have been sold and the money given to poor people."

But Jesus wasn't angry. He was pleased with Mary's gift. He knew she had done this because she loved Him. So Jesus said: "Don't scold Mary. Mary has done a good deed. She has shown how much she loves Me by giving Me this gift. From now on whenever men tell about Me, they will also tell about the good deed Mary has done."

When the Children Sang to Jesus

Matthew 21:1-11, 14-17

It was Sunday morning. Jesus and His friends were on their way to Jerusalem. They were going to the beautiful house of God, the temple.

When they came near to the city, Jesus told two of His helpers to go ahead and get a donkey. He was going to ride into the city just as kings did long ago.

The friends of Jesus went and found a donkey, just as Jesus had told them they would. They brought it to Jesus. Then they laid their coats on the donkey and set Jesus on it.

When the people in Jerusalem heard that Jesus was coming, they went out to meet Him. Some of them took off their fine coats and laid them on the road in front of Jesus. Others ran and pulled off branches from palm trees. They waved the branches like flags.

As the crowd walked along with Jesus toward the city, the people began singing a song of praise to Jesus. They said: "Blessed is He that comes in the name of the Lord. Hosanna in the highest!" That was their way of saying: "We praise Jesus! He is the Son of God, who is coming to save us. Hurrah!"

At last Jesus came to the big city, riding on the donkey. Some of the people went ahead; others followed Him. They kept on shouting and singing, "Hosanna, hosanna in the highest!" The streets were full of people. It was like a big parade.

Some strangers asked: "Who is the man riding on the donkey? Why are they singing for Him?" Those who knew Jesus answered: "This is Jesus, the Great Teacher." The happy crowd followed Jesus to the temple.

In the temple some children came and sang songs to Jesus. But the enemies of Jesus did not like to hear the children singing to Jesus. They said to Him: "Don't You hear what these children are saying? Why don't You tell them to be quiet?"

But Jesus liked the songs of the children. He would not stop them. He said to His enemies: "Don't you know that little children give God the best praise?"

When Jesus Washed His Disciples' Feet

John 13:3-15

"Clunk-clunk, clunk-clunk." The disciples took off their sandal shoes and dropped them on the floor. It had been a dusty trip from Bethany to Jerusalem. But now they were at the place where they were going to eat a special supper with Jesus.

Into an upstairs room they went. There they saw a table Peter and John had set. They also saw a water jug and a bowl and the towel they could use to wash their dusty, tired feet. They would have to help one another, though, because there was no servant there to do it.

"I'm tired," thought Andrew. "Let somebody else do it." "I'm hot," thought James. "Let somebody else do it." Before you knew it, they were all sitting at the table, and nobody had washed anyone else's dusty feet. Peter and John began to bring the food for the supper and still nobody offered to help.

Then Jesus got up from the table. He took off His robe and tied an apron around Himself. He took the water jug and poured some water into the bowl. Then He began to wash His disciples' feet and dried them with the towel.

The disciples felt ashamed when they saw Jesus doing this. After all, He was their Lord and Teacher. He shouldn't have to do a servant's work! So when Jesus came to Peter, Peter said: "Lord, I can't let You wash my feet."

Jesus said: "You won't get My love unless you do." When Peter heard this, he said: "Lord, wash not only my feet, but also my hands and my head."

When Jesus had finished washing all the disciples' feet, He put on His robe and sat down at the table again. The disciples were very quiet and ashamed. They were waiting to hear what Jesus would say.

"Do you know what I have done?" asked Jesus. "I have shown you how you ought to love one another. I am greater than you. I am your Lord. Yet I washed your feet. If you want to be My disciples, then you ought to love and serve one another, too."

The Lord's Supper

Luke 22:7-23; John 13:31 — 14:3

While Jesus was eating a last supper with His disciples before He died, He became very sad. He said to them: "Soon one of you will help my enemies to capture Me and kill Me."

The disciples looked at one another. They were surprised. "Who could do such a wicked thing?" they wondered. They became sad, too. One by one they asked Jesus: "Lord, is it I?"

Judas also asked: "Teacher, is it I?" Jesus answered him: "Yes. Do quickly what you're going to do." Then Judas got up from the table and went to tell the enemies of Jesus where they could catch Him.

When Judas was gone, Jesus took some bread. First He thanked His Father in heaven for it. Then He broke it into little pieces and gave it to His disciples. "Take, eat," He said. "This is My body, which is given for you. Do this in remembrance of Me."

Then Jesus took a cup of wine. After He thanked His Father in heaven for it, He passed the cup to His disciples. "Drink it, all of you," said Jesus. "This is My blood, which I am giving to take away your sins. Whenever you drink it, remember Me."

Jesus gave His disciples this special supper to show that He was going to die to take away people's sins. After He went back to heaven, they ate this Lord's Supper often together.

And whenever they ate the bread, they remembered how Jesus gave His body for them by dying on a cross. Whenever they drank the wine, they remembered how Jesus had shed His blood to wash away their sins.

Today, too, Jesus gives His disciples His body and His blood in the Lord's Supper. When the pastor gives the bread and wine in church, he says what Jesus said so long ago: "This is My body, which is given for you. This is My blood, which is shed for you."

Today, too, Jesus wants every Christian to be sure that He died for all people so that they could have God's forgiveness of sins. That's why the people who believe in Jesus go to His Supper often.

When Jesus Prayed in the Garden

Matthew 26:30-56; John 18:1-12

On the night before Jesus died, He took a walk with His friends after their last supper together. He led them to a garden called Gethsemane. When they came to the gate of the garden, He said: "Sit down here while I go and pray over there."

Then Jesus took His three best friends with Him into the garden. They were Peter, James, and John. "I feel very, very sad," He said to them. "Watch and pray so that you won't sin."

Then Jesus went away to a place where He could be alone. There He knelt down on the ground and prayed. He told His Father in heaven how hard it was for Him to suffer and die. But Jesus was willing to suffer and die to save all people from their sins. So He prayed, "Thy will be done."

While Jesus was praying, an angel from heaven came to Him. He told Jesus that our Father in heaven would help Him. Now Jesus felt strong enough to die.

After He prayed three times, Jesus came back to His friends. They were all sleeping, for it was late at night and they were tired and sad. So He woke them and said: "It is time for us to go." His enemies, who hated Him, were coming. They were coming with soldiers to capture Him.

Jesus knew that His enemies were coming, but He did not run away. He went out to meet them. He said to them: "For whom are you looking?" They said: "Jesus." Jesus answered: "I am He." When He said this, all the men fell down to the ground. Jesus showed them that He was stronger than they. But He let them get up again.

Now Judas, one of the disciples of Jesus, came up and gave Jesus a kiss. That was a signal for the soldiers to grab Jesus. Peter started to fight with his sword, but Jesus told him to stop it. "Shall I not do what My Father in heaven wants Me to do?" He asked.

Then Jesus let them tie His hands and make Him a prisoner. But all the friends of Jesus were afraid and ran away.

How Our Savior Suffered for Us

Matthew 27:1-31

All His life Jesus had been good to everybody. He loved the children and helped the sick people. But His enemies hated Him because He said He was their God and King. After His enemies captured Him in the Garden of Gethsemane, they took Him to a meeting. There they said: "Jesus must die!" Jesus let them keep Him as a prisoner.

Early the next morning they took Jesus to the house of Pontius Pilate. Pilate was the ruler of the Jews. He was also the judge who had to give them permission to kill Jesus. The enemies of Jesus wanted Pilate to say that they could hang Jesus on a cross. They also told lies about Jesus. They said: "Jesus is a bad man."

So Pilate took Jesus into his house and talked with Him. After a while he came out and told the people: "I can't find anything wrong with Jesus." But the crowd wanted to hang Jesus on a cross. They shouted: "Crucify Him! Crucify Him!"

Pilate was afraid to put Jesus to death. He knew that Jesus had done nothing wrong. But to please the people, Pilate told the soldiers to whip Jesus. So the soldiers took off His clothes and whipped Him with sticks and straps.

The soldiers also made fun of Jesus. They put an old purple coat on Him. They made a crown of thorns and pressed it on His head. They put a stick into His hands. Then they knelt down in front of Him. They did this because Jesus had said He was a king.

Jesus didn't say a word to those who were mean to Him. He suffered all this in order to pay for what we all do wrong.

After this Pilate showed Jesus to the people. He said to the people: "Look at the Man!" He thought they would feel sorry for Jesus when they saw how the soldiers had hurt Him. But the people shouted louder than before: "Crucify Him! Crucify Him!" At last Pilate called for some water and washed his hands. That meant he did not want to be the one who would kill Jesus. Then he told the soldiers to put Jesus on a cross, even though he knew Jesus had done nothing wrong.

When Jesus Died for Us

Matthew 27:31-56; John 19:17-37

Christians say, "Jesus suffered under Pontius Pilate." Pilate told his soldiers to hang Jesus on a cross. When the soldiers led Jesus through the streets and out of the city to the place where He was to die, a big crowd of people followed.

Some of the women along the way began to cry. Jesus turned to them and said: "Do not cry about Me, but cry about yourselves and your children." He meant that they should be sorry for all the sins which they and their children had done. He was suffering and dying to take away all the badness in people.

The soldiers took Jesus to a hill called Calvary. It was near the city of Jerusalem. There they nailed Him to a big wooden cross. Two robbers were also crucified with Jesus, one on each side of Him.

Jesus hung on the cross for a long time. He suffered much pain. But Jesus prayed for His enemies. He said: "Father, forgive them, for they know not what they do."

While Jesus was suffering on the cross, many people around the cross made fun of Him. They laughed and shouted. They said: "He saved others, but He cannot save Himself!" Some of them said: "If You are the Son of God, come down from the cross." But Jesus did not say a word. He was suffering in order to save those people, too.

One of the robbers believed that Jesus was the Savior. He said: "Lord remember me." Jesus said to him: "Today you will be with Me in heaven." After a while He said: "It is finished!" Then Jesus died. His work of saving people was done. He had paid for the sins of the whole world.

When Jesus died, the ground shook. Big rocks broke open. Many children of God who were dead became alive again. A large curtain in the temple tore apart from top to bottom. The captain of the soldiers near the cross of Jesus said: "Surely this was the Son of God."

That evening some friends of Jesus came and took down the body of Jesus from the cross. They wrapped it in clean cloth and laid it in a grave in a garden nearby. The grave was cut out of the side of a hill. They rolled a big stone in front of the grave and went home. They were sad because their dear Friend and Savior was dead.

The First Glad Easter Day

Matthew 28:8-10; John 20:18-23

On the first Easter morning some women came to the garden where Jesus' body had been buried. They were going to put some perfume on Jesus' body because they loved Him.

When they came to the grave, it was open. And when they came up to it they saw a young man sitting in the grave, dressed in white. He was a bright, shiny angel.

The angel said: "Don't be afraid. I know you are looking for Jesus. He is not here. He is risen. Go tell His friends that He is alive again."

So the women hurried home to tell the disciples what they had heard. On the way, who do you think met them? Yes, Jesus! As He came up to them, He said, "Hello!" And when the women saw it was really Jesus, they knelt down and touched His feet to show their love.

Then Jesus asked them to tell His friends to meet Him in the country where He used to live. So they hurried on their way and told their friends the wonderful news. How excited they all were!

That evening the friends of Jesus had a meeting in one of their homes. They were happy because Mary also had seen Jesus and had told them about it. But they were still afraid the enemies of Jesus would try to hurt them. So they locked all the doors in the house.

All at once Jesus was with them in the room. At first His friends were afraid when they saw Him. They thought they were seeing a ghost. But Jesus said: "Peace be with you." These words took away their fears.

Then Jesus showed them the marks from the nails that had been put through His hands. He also showed them the mark in His side where a soldier had stabbed Him. He even asked them to touch His hands and His feet. He wanted them to be sure He was really alive.

Now the friends of Jesus were sure that He was alive again, and they were very glad. Then Jesus said to them: "As My Father sent Me, even so send I you." He meant that they should be His helpers and should do His work from now on.

A Man Who Would Not Believe

John 20:19-31

Thomas, one of Jesus' disciples, was very sad. He had thought that Jesus was the promised Savior. He had expected Jesus to become a king. Now Thomas thought Jesus was dead without having saved His people.

While Thomas was sad and gloomy, some of the other disciples found him. "Thomas, Jesus is not dead. He is alive. We have seen Him," they told him excitedly. "It was evening. All of us disciples were together except you. Suddenly in the middle of the room stood Jesus, even though the doors were all locked. He said to us: 'Peace be to you.'"

Thomas shook his head. He would not believe them. He said: "I will not believe that Jesus is alive until I can put my finger into the marks the nails made in His hands and until I can touch the place where the soldier cut open His side with a spear."

A week passed by. Again the disciples were together in a room, with the doors closed. But this time Thomas was with them. Suddenly Jesus came again and said to them: "Peace be to you." Before they could say anything, Jesus called to Thomas and said: "Put your finger here and touch My hands, and put your hand into My side. Do not doubt, but believe."

Thomas touched Jesus' wounded hands and the side which had been hurt with a spear. He looked into the loving face of his Master, who he thought was dead. Oh, how sorry he was that he had not believed! And how glad he was that Jesus had come to show that He was alive!

Thomas fell down at Jesus' feet and cried: "My Lord and my God!" Now he was sure that Jesus was his Savior. Jesus said: "Thomas, because you have seen Me, you believe. But happy are they who have not seen and still believe." Thomas would have been happier if he had believed in the first place.

The Bible tells us that Jesus is living and that He is our Lord and Savior. Those who believe this are happy. They know that Jesus loves them and is with them even though they cannot see Him.